60 – DEAL

by
JAN KING

Illustrated by
CHARLES GOLL

CCC PUBLICATIONS

Published by

CCC Publications
1111 Rancho Conejo Blvd.
Suites 411 & 412
Newbury Park, CA 91320

Manufactured in the United States of America

Cover © 1996 CCC Publications

Interior illustrations © 1996 CCC Publications

Cover & interior art by Charles Goll

Cover/Interior production by Oasis Graphics

ISBN: 1-57644-023-0

If your local U.S. bookstore is out of stock, copies of this book may be obtained by mailing check or money order for $4.99 per book (plus $2.50 to cover postage and handling) to: CCC Publications, 1111 Rancho Conejo Blvd., Suites 411 & 412, Newbury Park, CA 91320

Pre-publication Edition - 8/96

"Now, where are those darn glasses? I just saw them
a few minutes ago!"

AT 60, YOU'RE EATING SO MUCH BRAN AND FIBER YOU NEED TO INSTALL A SEAT BELT ON YOUR TOILET.

"Oh my, Fred. When did our kneecaps shrink?"

WHEN YOU'RE 60, YOUR BATHROOM CONTAINS MORE LITERATURE THAN YOUR LIBRARY.

"Don't call me Grandma or you're dead meat, kid!"

WHEN YOU'VE HAD ONE TOO MANY FACE LIFTS.

EXERCISE 60'S STYLE!

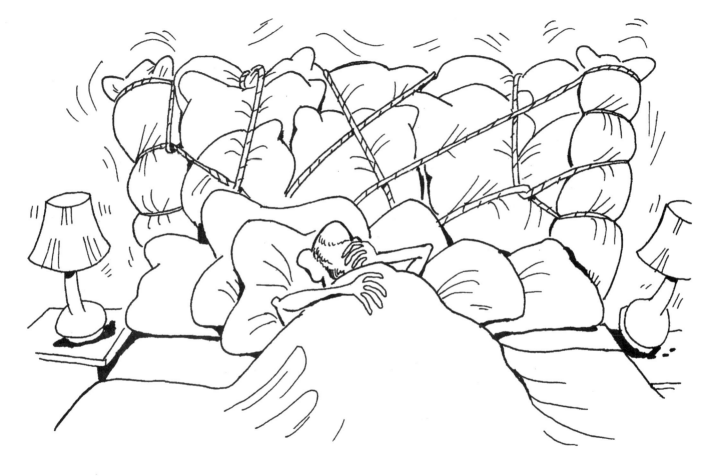

SAFE SEX AT 60 MEANS EXTRA PADDING ON YOUR HEADBOARD!

AT 60, YOU'VE DISCOVERED SURFIN'!

AT 60, YOU BECOME A CHARTER MEMBER OF THE HAIR CLUB FOR MEN.

AT 60, THE ONLY "BUNS OF STEEL" YOU'LL EVER HAVE
COME OUT OF YOUR OVEN.

"So Martha. Just how bad did you wreck the car?"

"Grandpa, did you ever see one of these <u>alive</u> when you were a kid?"

YOUR "KID" IS DEPRESSED ABOUT REACHING THE BIG 4-0!

"GETTING HIP" HAS AN ENTIRELY DIFFERENT MEANING TO A 60 YEAR OLD!

VEGAS ★ SPECI

THE "FIELD TRIP" – 60'S STYLE!

RETIRED: LET THE GAMES BEGIN!

AS YOU GET OLDER, YOUR DOCTORS SEEM TO GET
YOUNGER AND YOUNGER.

TRUMAN IS HARNESSING THE COSMIC ENERGY HE NEEDS FOR HIS OWN PERSONAL EXPANSION.

AT 60, YOU TAKE YOUR MEXICAN WITH A MAALOX CHASER!

"Don't you think you've overdone the 'Grecian Formula' thing just a bit?"

"No, no, no! You WILL NOT call the paramedics.
I don't care if it takes a month for the spasm to go away!"

"For goodness sakes June, what's with you?
I remember when we used to <u>do it</u> in the shower."

"Is that Muriel over there or is it Samsonite?"

AT 60, YOU HAVEN'T GOT THE TIME OR THE BREATH
TO BLOW OUT ALL YOUR CANDLES.

WANT TO LIVE? DON'T MESS WITH THE BINGOMEISTER!

THE 60'S MOBILE!

AT 60, YOU BECOME AN OFFICIAL SHAREHOLDER IN THE 3-M COMPANY!

YOU REFUSE TO BECOME VICTIMS OF THE "EMPTY NEST SYNDROME."

AT 60, YOU EAT YOUR DINNER WHEN YOU USED TO EAT YOUR LUNCH.

FOREPLAY AT 60: ENERGY CONSERVATION!

"Oh, Herb's O.K. This is what always happens when he spends the afternoon trying to play soccer with our grandkids."

"I'm giving Jack 'On The Job Training' for his new career after he retires next month."

"I think we should have gone to the South of France
when we were still in our twenties."

THE 60'S SOCIAL CALENDAR!

THE UPSIDE OF MENOPAUSE!

NEW YEAR'S EVE JUST AIN'T WHAT IT USED TO BE.

AT 60, YOU BOAST ABOUT YOUR BLOOD PRESSURE AND CHOLESTEROL INSTEAD OF YOUR SEX LIFE.

AT 60, A "FOOT FETISH" MEANS AN OBSESSION WITH DR. SCHOLL.

AT 60, YOUR LIFE BECOMES "THE DIET OF THE MONTH."

"But mom and dad, it's <u>July</u> for Pete's sake!"

"Grandpa, you've GOT to pick up the pace a little."

"Here, Melinda, put these on. Grandpa's 'playing plumber' again."

AT 60, VISITS WITH THE "CHILDREN" REQUIRE HEAVY MEDICATION.

"Margaret, don't you think it's about time you admit you need glasses?"

POWERWALKING AT 60!

AT 60, YOU START GETTING UP WITH THE CHICKENS!

AT 60, YOUR NEW OBSESSION BECOMES WATCHING THE WEATHER CHANNEL AND
REPORTING THE FORECAST TO ALL YOUR FRIENDS AND RELATIVES.

"Bill, can't I just read it to you?"

FASHION MUSTS FOR MEN AND WOMEN IN THEIR SIXTIES!

WILBUR CEREMONIOUSLY SALUTES THE BANK WHEN HIS MORTGAGE
IS FINALLY PAID OFF!

AT 60, YOU HAVE AMASSED ENOUGH TUPPERWARE TO STORE FOOD FOR AN ENTIRE NATION!

AT 60, IT'S JUST TOO DAMN MUCH TROUBLE TO LEARN
HOW TO PROGRAM THE VCR.

AFTER 60, LEAKY BLADDERS HAPPEN!

AT 60, YOU CAN FINALLY READ IN BED EVERY NIGHT
AND NOT BE INTERRUPTED.

AT 60, YOUR MOTTO BECOMES "RETIRE AND HIRE."

AFTER 60, FORGET HAVING ANYONE OVER FOR DINNER.

"I'm afraid Angela is not taking 60 very well at all."

NEW USE FOR THE RETIRED MAN!

AT 60 YOUR OBSESSION WITH CALISTHENICS
BECOMES AN OBSESSION WITH CLEAVAGE.

AT 60, YOU'VE GOT MORE LOVE THAN EVER BEFORE!

TITLES BY CCC PUBLICATIONS

Retail $4.99
"?" book
POSITIVELY PREGNANT
WHY MEN ARE CLUELESS
CAN SEX IMPROVE YOUR GOLF?
THE COMPLETE BOOGER BOOK
FLYING FUNNIES
MARITAL BLISS & OXYMORONS
THE VERY VERY SEXY ADULT DOT-TO-DOT BOOK
THE DEFINITIVE FART BOOK
THE COMPLETE WIMP'S GUIDE TO SEX
THE CAT OWNER'S SHAPE UP MANUAL
PMS CRAZED: TOUCH ME AND I'LL KILL YOU!
RETIRED: LET THE GAMES BEGIN
THE OFFICE FROM HELL
FOOD & SEX
FITNESS FANATICS
YOUNGER MEN ARE BETTER THAN RETIN-A
BUT OSSIFER, IT'S NOT MY FAULT

Retail $4.95
YOU KNOW YOU'RE AN OLD FART WHEN...
1001 WAYS TO PROCRASTINATE
HORMONES FROM HELL II
SHARING THE ROAD WITH IDIOTS
THE GREATEST ANSWERING MACHINE
  MESSAGES OF ALL TIME
WHAT DO WE DO NOW?? (A Guide For New
Parents)
HOW TO TALK YOU WAY OUT OF
  A TRAFFIC TICKET
THE BOTTOM HALF (How To Spot Incompetent
  Professionals)
LIFE'S MOST EMBARRASSING MOMENTS
HOW TO ENTERTAIN PEOPLE YOU HATE

YOUR GUIDE TO CORPORATE SURVIVAL
THE SUPERIOR PERSON'S GUIDE TO EVERYDAY
  IRRITATIONS
GIFTING RIGHT

Retail $5.95
LOVE DAT CAT
CRINKLED 'N' WRINKLED
SIGNS YOU'RE A GOLF ADDICT
SMART COMEBACKS FOR STUPID QUESTIONS
YIKES! IT'S ANOTHER BIRTHDAY
SEX IS A GAME
SEX AND YOUR STARS
SIGNS YOUR SEX LIFE IS DEAD
40 AND HOLDING YOUR OWN
50 AND HOLDING YOUR OWN
MALE BASHING: WOMEN'S FAVORITE PASTIME
THINGS YOU CAN DO WITH A USELESS MAN
MORE THINGS YOU CAN DO WITH A
  USELESS MAN
THE WORLD'S GREATEST PUT-DOWN LINES
LITTLE INSTRUCTION BOOK OF THE
  RICH & FAMOUS
WELCOME TO YOUR MIDLIFE CRISIS
GETTING EVEN WITH THE ANSWERING MACHINE
ARE YOU A SPORTS NUT?
MEN ARE PIGS / WOMEN ARE BITCHES
ARE WE DYSFUNCTIONAL YET?
TECHNOLOGY BYTES!
50 WAYS TO HUSTLE YOUR FRIENDS ($5.99)
HORMONES FROM HELL
HUSBANDS FROM HELL
KILLER BRAS & Other Hazards Of The 50's
IT'S BETTER TO BE OVER THE HILL
  THAN UNDER IT
HOW TO REALLY PARTY!!!

WORK SUCKS!
THE PEOPLE WATCHER'S FIELD GUIDE
THE UNOFFICIAL WOMEN'S DIVORCE GUIDE
THE ABSOLUTE LAST CHANCE DIET BOOK
FOR MEN ONLY (How To Survive Marriage)
THE UGLY TRUTH ABOUT MEN
NEVER A DULL CARD
RED HOT MONOGAMY
  (In Just 60 Seconds A Day) ($6.95)
HOW TO SURVIVE A JEWISH MOTHER ($6.95)
WHY MEN DON'T HAVE A CLUE ($7.99)
LADIES, START YOUR ENGINES! ($7.99)

Retail $3.95
NO HANG-UPS
NO HANG-UPS II
NO HANG-UPS III
HOW TO SUCCEED IN SINGLES BARS
HOW TO GET EVEN WITH YOUR EXES
TOTALLY OUTRAGEOUS BUMPER-SNICKERS
($2.95)

NO HANG-UPS – CASSETTES Retail $4.98

Vol. I:	GENERAL MESSAGES (Female)
Vol. I:	GENERAL MESSAGES (Male)
Vol. II:	BUSINESS MESSAGES (Female)
Vol. II:	BUSINESS MESSAGES (Male)
Vol. III:	'R' RATED MESSAGES (Female)
Vol. III:	'R' RATED MESSAGES (Male)
Vol. IV:	SOUND EFFECTS ONLY
Vol. V:	CELEBRI-TEASE